Speaking Better French

WITHDRAWN

Faux Amis

**Why saying *sensible* isn't sensible,
and why you should <u>never</u> say there
are *préservatifs* in your food.**

Saul H. Rosenthal

Speaking Better French: Faux Amis

Published by Wheatmark™
610 East Delano Street, Suite 104, Tucson, Arizona 85705 U.S.A.
www.wheatmark.com

ISBN-13: 978-1-58736-732-8
ISBN-10: 1-58736-732-7
LCCN: 2006936844

Also written by Saul H. Rosenthal:

The Rules for the Gender of French Nouns

Acknowledgements

I wish to specially thank Annick Michot, Catherine Ostrow and Sylvie Shurgot who each read part of the manuscript and helped me find errors. I also wish to thank my daughter Sadie and many of my French friends who patiently answered my questions about French usage. Finally, I'd like to thank my wife, Cindy, who was very patient during all the time I invested in writing this book. I really appreciated her support throughout.

Contents

Introduction

I wrote this book to help you avoid possible awkward mis-understandings when you encounter *faux amis*, those confusing word pairs which appear the same in French and English but which can have problematically different meanings.

You can find lists of *faux amis* in lots of places. This is not a list. What I have tried to do is to write an easy-to-read book in conversational language. It's not meant to be a textbook either. I want you to be able to read it for fun, and I hope that you will find it to be fascinating.

I have tried to explain the nuances and to give lots of examples so that you will understand the differences in usage between French and English. The examples will help you understand how the words **can** be used, but I also have tried to make clear how they **shouldn't** be used.

When you have finished reading this book, I hope that you will have learned most of the *faux amis* without having consciously memorized them.

I intentionally didn't alphabetize the words. This is not a dictionary either. I wanted to make reading the book a discovery, so that you will stumble on interesting words you didn't expect to encounter. I've tried to make the book a pleasure for you to read—especially if you have an inquisitive mind.

I did, however, put an alphabetized index in the back of the book for reference.

I also have included a bit of history of a number of the words, with the aim of making your reading more interesting.

Now let's go on and discuss a little more about what *faux amis* are:

Faux amis, or "false friends," are "friends" because they look the same in English and in French. They have similar spelling. Frequently they may be spelled exactly the same!

They are "false" friends, however, because they don't mean the same thing! The French word may look just like the English word, but it may mean something else entirely.

One way these *faux amis* can cause trouble for you is if you misunderstand them when you hear them or see them written. It's easy to assume that a French word means the same when it looks and sounds pretty much the same as an English word.

However a *faux ami* can cause you even more trouble, and sometimes even embarrassment, when you use it in conversation and it means something different than what you expected. You assume you know what it means because it looks just like an English word. Unfortunately, however, as I've said, it sometimes means something else entirely than what you actually meant to say.

My wife likes to recount a classic example of this kind of misunderstanding that happened to her personally. She was discussing food with French friends and mentioned that there are often preservatives in the food that you buy at the supermarkets. She used the word *préservatifs*. However *préservatifs* doesn't mean preservatives in French, it means condoms! You can imagine the looks on the faces of her friends in hearing that there are often condoms in supermarket food.

This problem of *faux amis* is pretty much restricted to French. You won't find the same thing if you are studying Russian or German, for instance. There are so many every-day French and English words that are almost identical that you come to expect that similar words mean the same thing. After discovering that *similar* means similar, *différent* means different, *stupide* means stupid, and *intelligent* means intelligent, it comes as a surprise when *sensible* doesn't mean sensible.

Faux amis are words like *préservatifs* and *sensible*. They are words that are recognizible as English words and that we welcome as old friends, but which turn out to have different meanings in French. They can leave French people looking very perplexed when we use them erroneously with an English meaning.

In order to be fooled by "false friends" you have to have the legitimate expectation that a French word which looks and sounds like an English word will actually have the same meaning as the English word. The truth is that it is a very legitimate expectation. In conversation I have often used an English word, pronounced it with a French accent, and successfully had it understood by my French friends. In fact, they sometimes remark on how good my French vocabulary is because I use words that they wouldn't expect a foreigner to know. I can't take credit for it honestly, so I explain that the rather esoteric French word that I just used is really a rather esoteric English word too.

To demonstrate how many words do mean the same thing, and why it is easy to be fooled when a French word does not have the same meaning as the English, here is a short list of paired words which do mean the same thing. I found them just by starting at the letter A of my dictionary:

abandon- abandon

abandonné - abandonned

abandonner- to abandon

abaque - abacus

abattoir - abattoir

abbaye - abbey

abbesse - abbess

abcès - abcess

abdication - abdication

abdiquer - to abdicate

abdomen - abdomen

abdominal - abdominal

abducteur - abductor

aberrant - aberrant

aberration - aberration

abhorrer - to abhor

abject - abject

abjuration - abjuration

abjurer - to abjure

ablation - ablation

ablution -ablution

abnégation - abnegation

abolir - to abolish

aboli - abolished

abolitionniste - abolitionist

abominable - abominable

abomination - abomination

abominer - to abominate

abondance - abundance

abondamment - abundantly

Believe it or not, this whole list came from just the first two pages of the A's in my dictionary! I was still in words starting with Ab.

Imagine the length of the list if I had gone through all the rest of the A's, never mind the whole dictionary, (which had over 900 pages). It gives you an idea how related the two languages are.

There's a good reason for the similarity between English and

French. It's important to remember that after the conquest of England in 1066 by William the Conqueror, the language of the ruling classes and the court was French for hundreds of years after. Richard the Lionhearted, for example, although King of England, didn't speak a word of English. His language was French. English was the language of the conquered Anglo-Saxons, the lower classes and the rural people.

Because the ruling class spoke French for some hundreds of years, a great many French words became incorporated into English. Indeed, what we now call English is an amalgam of the original Anglo Saxon language and the French of the conquerors (plus a lot of other miscellaneous words that were added later, like pizza and taco).

In fact, when talking of these English words that are identical, or almost identical to French, we say that they come from French. However, they don't just "come from" French! They are French, as we have just seen. Some of my French friends joke that English is just French mispronounced.

Then why are some words *faux amis*? Why do they look like English words but have different meanings? The answer comes from the fact that these French words entered English such a long time ago. They have often had hundreds of years to grow apart. Sometimes the English meaning of a word has gradually changed, sometimes it has been the French meaning.

Many, many words are still practically overlapping in meaning in French and in English. That is to say that they still mean just about the same things, and you can use the French word almost every time you would use the English word. For example, *abhorrer* and to abhor.

Some words have parted ways only slightly. Words like this still tend to overlap in some usages even though parts of their sense now differ.

There will be other words that have grown apart over the centuries so that their meanings are now different, but it's still evident that they came from the same ancestor.

Other words, although they may be written identically, or almost identically, may now have taken completely different meanings, for example *sympathique* and sympathetic.

Other words, as you will discover, may look and be spelled exactly the same and have come from the same (French) stem, but may now have completely different—or even opposite—meanings. For example *inhabitable* and inhabitable.

Finally, some words, although they look alike, will have come from different directions and different stems, and have unrelated meanings. For example, *dérider* and to deride.

English speakers usually recognize recently transplanted words like rendez-vous and entrée as French words. However, they are not often aware that so many of the common words they use in everyday speech are also French.

It's also interesting to reflect on the fact that numerous English words are just fragments of French word complexes, washed up on the shore of our language, so to speak.

For example, consider the English word "lassitude" which doesn't seem related in stem to any other English word with a similar meaning. Where does it come from?

It makes more sense when you know that in French there is a

transitive verb *lasser*, which means to tire out or weary. *Cela me lasse* means "That tires me out" The adjective *las/lasse* means tired, and *lassant* means tiring.

Finally, in this group of French words, is the noun *lassitude*, which, not surprisingly, means lassitude in French as well as in English. Thus, it's not a mysterious word, coming out of nowhere. It comes straight from French, a little orphan which got into English without the company of the rest of its family of *lasser, las, lassant,* etc.

There are many similar words all around us. Some are fairly obviously French sounding, and have come relatively recently into English—like *sabotage* and *saboteur*, members of the French family of words related to the verb *saboter*. Others are more like lassitude, words you would think of as pure English words.

It's interesting to reflect that in recent years there has been a reversal in the direction of word migration. As English has become the "global language," many English words have been incorporated into French. For example *parking, shopping,* and *weekend* are now all in common use in France, and the stop signs in France say STOP, rather than ARRÊT.

Let's go on now to investigate some of our *faux amis*.

Faux Amis

I have purposely not alphabetized these faux amis. I do not mean this to be a dictionary, but rather an intriguing book of discovery. My hope is that, while reading it, you will stumble unsuspectingly upon a multitiude of interesting words that you didn't expect to encounter.

Please note that some words have many, many minor meanings, both in English and in French, and that I don't make any attempt to list them all, but I try instead to restrict the discussion to those senses of the word that are in common use.

I have not tried to include all faux amis, but have tried to include the important ones that you are likely to encounter. It is certainly possible that you will find others not included in this book.

Now, let's get started.

sensible - **sensible**

The word *sensible* in French means sensitive, either sensitive physically or sensitive emotionally.

Sensible isn't related to the idea of "making good sense"

as in English. It's related to sensing and sensation and thus, coming from a different direction, it has a completely different meaning.

> *L'oreille humaine est moins sensible à certains sons.*

> *Vous êtes trop sensible.*

> *Il est toujours sensible à son charme.*

Sensible also means perceptible as in "able-to-be-sensed."

> *La différence de coloration était à peine sensible.*

Sensible does **not** mean "sensible." To say sensible you'd use *sensé* or *raisonnable.*

> *C'est une idée bien sensée/raisonnable.*

Conversely, *insensible* means insensitive or imperceptible, as in:

> *Un homme dur et insensible.* - insensitive

> *Il est insensible au charme des femmes* - insensitive

> *La différence était presque insensible.* - imperceptible

la déception **- the deception**
décevoir **- to deceive**

The noun *la déception* means the disappointment.

> *Quand je suis revenu c'était une cruelle décep-*
> *tion* - it was a cruel disappointment

The verb *décevoir* means to disappoint.

> *J'étais très déçu.* - disappointed

La déception does **not** mean "the deception." To say the deception you'd use *la tromperie* or *la supercherie.*

Décevoir does **not** mean "to deceive." To say "I was deceived" you'd use *J'ai été trompé.*

Interestingly, there **are** French words *désappointement, désappointer,* and *désappointé,* that exist and that do mean disappointment, to disappoint, and disappointed, respectively. However these words are rarely used compared to *déception, décevoir,* and *déçu.*

terrible - **terrible**

Terrible means terrible, dreadful, awful, as in English:

> *L'accident a été terrible.*

However, in informal language it can also mean the opposite: terrific, fantastic. You can usually tell by context and tone of voice. If someone says about a meal or a wine,

> *Ce vin n'est pas terrible.*

or, in more casual language, what the French call *la langue familière:*

> *C'est pas terrible !*

it means he **didn't** like it.

assister - **to assist**
l'assistance - **the assistance**

As you would expect, *assister quelqu'un* does mean to assist someone, as in:

> *J'ai assisté mon père dans son travail.*

> *L'infirmière assiste le chirugien.*

> *Nous étions là hier pour assister Jean.*

There is also the sense of assisting someone emotionally:

> *J'ai assisté ma mère dans ses derniers moments.*

However, the most common use of *assister* has a different meaning. Usually, *assister à* means to be present at or to attend, as in:

> *J'ai assisté à une conférence hier.*

> *Nous allons assister à l'opéra.*

Remember that *J'ai assisté à une conference* does **not** mean you assisted the conference in any way.

Similarly, *l'assistance* means the audience (opera) or the people present (conference), as well as assistance in the sense of "aid."

avertissement - **advertisement**

An *avertissement* is a warning or refers to alerting someone or letting them know in advance. It comes from the
verb *avertir* and has nothing to do with advertising.

> *Je ne faisais pas attention à ses sages avertisse-
> ments* - I didn't pay attention to his sensible
> warnings.

If you want to say an advertisement use *une réclame* or
une publicité.

malicieux - **malicious**
malice - **malice**

The meanings of *malicieux* and *malice* have changed in
French to mean mischievious and mischieviousness with
an implication of cleverness.

Malice and *malicieux* used to mean malice and malicious,
but the French language has evolved and these meanings have mostly become obsolete in modern French,
although you still may encounter the old meanings in clas-
sical works. *Malicieux* has come to mean mischievious
and sometimes a little teasing. Interestingly, the original
meanings endure in English.

Thus:

> *un enfant vif et malicieux*
>
> *un chaton malicieux*

If you want to say malicious in French say *méchant* or

malveillant avec préméditation. **For** malice use *méchanceté* **or** *malveillance.*

> There is malice in her remarks - *Il y a de la malveillance dans ses propos.*

> She said that to you with malice - *Elle l'a dit avec la préméditation de te blesser.*

chagrin - **chagrin**

Chagrin in French means sorrow or grief.

Chagrin in English means annoyance, disappointment, frustration, and even humiliation.

To translate: "He was chagrined at his failure," use *Il était déçu, contrarié et humilié . . .*

Several centuries ago, *chagrin* in French also had the meaning of irritation and annoyance, but this meaning has become obsolete in current usage. It's interesting though, because, like so many other examples, it demonstrates the common ancestry of the two words.

hardi - **hardy**

Hardi means bold and daring in French.

Hardy used to have the same meaning in English but that meaning has largely dropped out of current usage. In English, as you know, hardy now means strong, resilient, and capable of withstanding stress.

To say hardy in French, you'd say *robuste* or *résistant*.

"Foolhardy," meaning foolishly or overly bold, is left over from when hardy meant bold in English too. It comes from the Old French *folhardi*. (*fol* = crazy or foolish, *hardi* = bold)

un préservatif - **a preservative**

Un préservatif in French is a condom!

If you want to talk about a preservative, in food for example, say *un conservateur*, or *un agent de conservation*. If you say, *"Il y a beaucoup de préservatifs dans la nourriture,"* people will look at you very, very strangely!

pétulant - **petulant**
pétulance - **petulance**

While in English, petulant means childishly irascible and sulky, in French it means bubbly and exhuberant. (It may be related to *pétillant* or bubbly, as in *un vin pétillant*).

Pétulance means exhuberance.

To say the English word petulant in French use *irascible*.

To say the English word petulance use *irascibilité*.

sympathie - **sympathy**
sympathique - **sympathetic**

Sympathie doesn't mean sympathy in current French, it

means a warm spontoneous feeling of affinity that one person feels for another, (although in literary French it can be a synonym for sympathy).

Sympathique doesn't mean sympathetic, it means likeable, warm, agreeable, nice, pleasant. If you say:

> *Je le trouve très sympathique.*

it means that you find him a very warm, likeable person. *Sympathique* is often abbreviated in common speech as "sympa." For example:

> *Il est très sympa.*

Sympathique is not restricted to talking about a person. It can also be used to refer to an object, as in:

> *Ce petit restaurant est très sympa.*

If you want to say the English word sympathy in French, use *compassion*.

To say the English word sympathetic in French, you can use *compréhensif* which means understanding, or try *compatissant*, which is stronger and more like actively sympathetic. Finally, you can say:

> *Il a de la compassion.*

To say sympathize with in French, use *compatir à*.

compréhensif - comprehensive

In English the adjective comprehensive usually means complete or exhaustive.

In French *compréhensif* is also an adjective but it relates to *comprendre* and means understanding.

Il est très compréhensif et sympathique.

If you want to say the English word comprehensive in French, use *complet et exhaustif.*

l'occasion - the occasion

L'occasion means the occasion or opportunity in English and in French. However, in French *une occasion* has a second meaning of a bargain as in:

J'ai trouvé une vraie occasion hier!

Probably the most common usage however, of occasion in French, is to refer to something second hand as in:

Une voiture d'occasion.

Le camion n'est pas neuf, c'est une occasion.

une location - a location

The meanings of these two nouns are completely unrelated. In English a location is a place. In French *une location* refers to a rental.

Location de voitures ici. - Cars for rent here.

Une voiture de location. - A rental car.

Nous avons trouvé une location pour nos vacances. - We found a rental (house) for our vacation.

Remember that *C'est une jolie location* **doesn't** mean that it's a pretty location. It means that it's a pretty rental. To say that it's a pretty location you'd use *un joli endroit*.

un raisin - a raisin

Un raisin in French is a grape. In English it's a dried grape.

To refer to a dried grape, or what we would call a raisin, you should use *un raisin sec*.

une prune - a prune

This is a similar *faux ami*. Une prune in French is a plum.

To refer to what we would call a prune, use *un pruneau*.

As an aside, in French slang *un pruneau* can also refer to a bullet or "slug."

Gare aux pruneaux ! - Watch out for the bullets!

importer - to import

In English, to import means to bring goods into the country.

Another meaning in a literary sense is to mean or signify, as in:

> The arrival of cheap steel imports trouble for the steel industry.

While, in French, *importer* does mean to import or bring into the country (as in English), it does not have the second English meaning (to signify).

However, *importer* has a third meaning which is seen very commonly: to be important, to matter.

> *Il importe qu'il arrive à l'heure* - It's important that he arrives on time.

> *Peu m'importe.* - It doesn't matter to me.

Import can be used as a noun with this meaning in English:

> It's of little import to me.

However the sentence *Il importe qu'il arrive à l'heure* looks very foreign to us. That's because the meaning "to be important" is now archaic for the verb "to import" in English.

inhabitable - **inhabitable**
inhabité - **inhabited**

You can't ask for a better example of a *faux ami* than this. *Inhabitable* and inhabitable are spelled exactly the same, but they are opposites!

Inhabitable doesn't mean inhabitable. It means **not** *habitable* or uninhabitable. To say the English word inhabitable (able to be lived in) in French, use *habitable*.

Similarly, *inhabité* doesn't mean inhabited, it means uninhabited. To say the English word inhabited (lived in), use *habité*.

To review, as this is a bit confusing:

> To say the English word inhabitable in French, say *habitable*.
>
> To say the English word **un**inhabitable in French, say *inhabitable*.
>
> To say the English word inhabited in French, say *habité*.
>
> To say the English word **un**inhabited in French, say *inhabité*.

harassé - **harassed**
harassant - **harassing**

> *Harassé* in French means exhausted, and *harassant* means exhausting.
>
> *Cette tâche est harassante.*
>
> Remember: *Je suis vraiment harassé* **doesn't** mean "I'm being really harassed." It means "I'm really exhausted."
>
> If you want to say the English word "to harass" in French use *harceler*. For harassing, use *harcelant*.

actuel - **actual**
actuellement - **actually**
actualité - **actuality**

Actuel/actuelle is a real *faux ami*. It doesn't mean actual at all. It's an adjective and it means current, existing now.

> *Votre consommation actuelle est...* - Your amount consumed (used) as of now is...

> *La situation actuelle est grave* - The current situation is grave.

Actuellement means currently, presently.

> *Il est actuellement à Paris* - He is in Paris right now.

L'actualité has to do with the topicality or the currentness of (a bit of news, an idea, a book, etc.). *Les actualités* are the news or the current events.

Remember that *en l'état actuel des choses* **doesn't** mean "in the actual state of things" or "in the real state of things." Those phrases in English imply a possibility of permanence—that that's the way things are, have been, and will continue to be.

On the other hand, *en l'état actuel des choses* **does** mean "in the present state of things." It describes a transient state—and allows the possibility that it wasn't that way in the past and that it may not be that way in the future

If you want an equivalent for actual in French use *réel*.

To say the English word actually in French, use *en fait* or *en réalité*.

cajoler - to cajole

In English to cajole means to persuade or seduce someone into doing something by coaxing and flattery.

In French *cajoler* means to surround someone with affectionate attention and tender words, to baby or cuddle someone. (Over the centuries it has lost its negative sense of attempting to persuade.)

If you really want to say the English word cajole in French, use *enjôler*.

dérider - to deride

Dérider has a very different meaning than to deride. It means to make someone less worried and sad, to cheer them up. (It comes from the literal meaning of *dé-rider*, or to remove the *rides*, or wrinkles, from the persons forehead.)

> *Je vais essayer de la dérider.*

> *Il était triste hier, mais aujourd'hui il s'est déridé.*

If you want to use the English verb "to deride" in French, use *ridiculiser, railler,* or *se moquer de.*

dérivatif - **derivative**

Un *dérivatif* in French is a distraction or a tension release.

> *Il utilise le sport comme dérivatif.*

If you want to say the English word derivative use *un dérivé* (which comes from *dériver de* or " to derive from"). For example :

> *C'est un dérivé du pétrole.*

vicieux/vicieuse - **vicious**

In French *vicieux* is related to vice rather than to cruelty, violence, or dangerousness, as in English. *Vicieux* means depraved or perverted.

> *Il faut être un peu vicieux pour aimer ce film.*

To come close to vicious use *méchant, malveillant,* or *violent* according to the sense in English.

(It's interesting to note that vicious used to mean depraved in English as well, coming from its French roots, but it has evolved a different meaning and the meaning "depraved" has since become obsolete.)

officieux/officieuse - **officious**
or
officieux/officieuse - **official**

Officieux is a really interesting word. Officious means

pompous, bossy and petty in English. *Officieux* doesn't mean anything like that in French.

You might expect that, in that case, *officieux* might mean official. Actually, *officieux* means exactly the opposite—or unofficial—as in:

> *une conclusion officieuse* - an unofficial conclusion

Remember that *une réunion officieuse* isn't an official meeting, it's an unofficial one.

Similarly, *officieusement* means unofficially, as in:

> *Je peux le dire, mais officieusement.*

If you want to say the English adjective "official" in French, use *officiel*.

If you want to say the English word "officious" in French use something like *autoritaire, pompeux* or *suffisant*, (or a combination of similar words, depending on context).

(Interestingly, in the past the English word "officious" used to mean "unofficial" in diplomatic language, showing its derivation from *officieux*).

formel - **formal**
formellement - **formally**

The first meaning of the English word "formal" is official, ceremonial, dressy, solemn, if you are talking about an occasion. If you are talking about a person, formal can mean stiff, conservative and perhaps pompous.

Formel **does not** have these meanings in French. *Formel* **doesn't** mean official, ceremonial, or stiff.

Other meanings of the English word "formal" are according to form, as in "a formal request" or "formal training," and just for form, as in "It's a purely formal arrangement,"

Formel can also have these same general meanings in French. For example, *Un arrangement purement formel.*

However, the way *formel* is usually used in French is to describe an order, a denial, a statement, a proof, etc, and it means unequivocal, clear, precise, categorical, certain, incontestable, undeniable, or irrefutable, (as in a categorical denial, a strict proof, or a precise order).

> *un démenti formel* - a total denial, a flat denial

> *une preuve formelle* - a strict/incontestable proof

> *Je suis formel.* - I'm absolutely certain.

> *Défense formelle d'entrer* - entrance is strictly forbidden

Similarly, the word formally in English usually means ceremoniously or officially, (although it can mean according to form as in "I'd like to formally request...").

In French, however, *formellement* means unequivocally, strictly or categorically.

> *Il est formellement interdit de fumer/entrer.*

If you are referring to something like an occasion or a restaurant, and you want to say that it is formal in the sense of dressy and ceremonial, use *cérémonieux* or *solennel*.

If you are talking about a person and you want to say that he or she is formal, or has a formal style or a formal air about him, use *compassé, guindé, empesé,* or *formaliste*.

If you are talking about clothes or a style of dress, and you want to say they are formal in the sense of "dressy," use *habillé*. If you want to say that the clothes are dressy and that you especially like them, say that they are *chic* or *élégant*.

Note that *habillé* doesn't mean "formal" like tuxedos and formal gowns, it just means "dressy." *Plus habillé* means dressier, and you can use other terms like *un peu habillé* or *très habillé*.

caméra - **camera**

The French word *caméra* refers just to a movie or TV camera. For a personal camera that we are most likely to call a "camera," the French say *un appareil photo*.

The French will probably understand if you say camera, but it's not the right word.

consistant - **consistent**

The English word consistent can have at least three shades of meaning.

The first meaning is unchanging, as in "consistent results," or "a consistent approach."

The second meaning is in agreement with or compatible with, as in "results consistent with the theory," or "symptoms consistent with the diagnosis."

The third meaning is being logical and not self-contradictory, as in "a consistent argument."

The French word *consistant* doesn't have any of these meanings at all. *Consistant* means having substance, firm, solid, substantial. It usually refers to a substance, a food or a meal. If used for a sauce it would be translated as thick. It can also be used figuratively for a film plot, for instance, meaning that the plot has substance to it.

Likewise, *inconsistant* means insubstantial or lacking substance.

When it refers to a sauce or a cream *inconsistant* could be translated as thin or runny. For a plot, a film, a novel or an accusation it is used figuratively, and also means flimsy and without substance. It is **not** a synonym for the English word inconsistent, which means not holding together logically.

reporter - **to report**
le report - **the report**

In French, *reporter* **never** means to report. It is related in stem to *porter*, (to carry). It means *re-porter*, thus to carry back or to bring back an object.

More often, reporter has a figurative meaning and means to carry back in time, as in:

> *Cela me reporte à ma jeunesse.*

Reporter can also mean to put off, postpone, or carry into the future as in:

> *La réunion a été reportée à jeudi prochain.*

It can also mean to transfer (literally: "to carry to"), as affection:

> *Après le décès de sa femme il a reporté toute son affection sur sa fille.*

Finally, in accounting, it can mean to carry forward, as in:

> *Il faut reporter cette somme.*

Similarly, *le report* doesn't mean the report. It refers to the carrying forward of a sum in accounting, or the postponement of a meeting or *rendez-vous*. To say the report in French use *le rapport*.

intoxication - **intoxication**
intoxiquer - **to intoxicate**
intoxiqué - **intoxicated**

In English these words most usually refer to drinking an excess of alcohol. In French, on the other hand, the noun *intoxication* comes from "toxin" or "toxic" and means poisoning. In familiar speech it also means brainwashing, such as by the press or the media.

Similarly, the verb *intoxiquer* means to poison, or to brainwash.

The adjective *intoxiqué* means poisoned or suffering from poison. It can also mean addicted. When used as a noun, *un intoxiqué* is an addict.

Remember, *intoxication* does **not** refer to drunkenness. If you want an equivalent to the English adjective drunk, in French, use *ivre, soûl* or *gris*.

For drunkenness, as a noun referring to the state of having had too much to drink, use *ivresse*. For chronic drunkenness use *ivrognerie*.

Although in English you can say "intoxicated with love" or "intoxicated with the beauty of the countryside," meaning drunk or euphoric with love, or beauty, those expressions don't work in French. In French *intoxiqué* has a definite negative connotation. On the other hand you can say "drunk with love" as in English by using *ivre* or *grisé*.

disgracieux/disgracieuse - **disgraceful**

This is fairly straightforward:

Disgracieux means ungraceful or awkward. *Disgracieux* does **not** mean disgraceful.

If you want to say the English word disgraceful in French, use *honteux, scandaleux* or *infâme*.

(However, just to confuse things, *une disgrâce* **does** mean a disgrace in French, and *disgracié* **does** mean disgraced or in disgrace, but it is little used).

Il est tombé en disgrâce.

gracieux/gracieuse - **gracious**

Similarly, while the French adjective *gracieux/gracieuse* can mean gracious, it usually means graceful. There is a third possible meaning, as well. When someone says *à titre gracieux*, it means free, gratis, complimentary.

If you want to say gracious in French, other, non-ambiguous, words that you can use are *charmant, poli, affable* or *courtois*.

As an adverb, *gracieusement* means gracefully or graciously.

And there is a noun, *la grâce*, which means grace, charm, or gracefulness—all three.

marron - **maroon**

The color *marron* in French is chestnut brown, while the color maroon in English is in the red family. (The French word comes from *un marron*, which is a chestnut).

suffisant - **sufficient**

The French word *suffisant* does mean sufficient.

C'est plus que suffisant pour nous.

However it has a second meaning. It also means self-important, arrogant, conceited.

Il parle avec un air très suffisant.

mondain/mondaine - **mundane**

Mondain is a French adjective that means fashionable or having to do with high society. For example:

une soirée mondaine

un homme mondain

The English word mundane is almost the opposite as it means ordinary and down-to-earth.

There was a second meaning of *mondain* in French which is now fairly obsolete. In an old religious context *mondain* meant worldly or earthly as opposed to sacred. (Referring to earthly pleasures, for example). It derived undoubtedly from the word *le monde* or the world.

It is interesting to speculate that the English word mundane probably came from this older meaning of *mondain*, as worldly. This was likely to have been the original sense of the word which migrated into English, while "having to do with high society," which *mondain* means today, is probably a later evolution in French.

Un mondain/une mondaine is also a noun, meaning a person in the world of high society.

As an odd euphemism, *la police mondaine* is the vice squad!

demander - **to demand**
une demande - **a demand**

As you probably already know, *demander* means simply to ask or request. It has none of the implication of insistence, authority, or harshness that it has in English. Thus:

> *Je lui ai demandé son avis.*

> *Puis-je vous demander de parler plus lentement ?*

Demander can also mean to need or require, but with a much softer connotation than in English:

> *Cela demande toute mon attention.*

If you want an equivalent to the English word "to demand," use *insister*, or, even better, use *exiger*, which is stronger.

Similarly, une demande is usually a simple request:

> *J'ai fait une demande de renseignements.* (I asked for information.)

> *Il l'a demandée en mariage.* (He asked for her hand in marriage.)

> *Cela est cuisiné sur demande.* (That dish is prepared on demand.)

In economics, *la demande* is the demand from "supply and demand."

> *La demande d'acier a diminué.*

In law, *une demande* is a petition (for divorce, for example) or a claim (for damages, etc).

Son mari a fait une demande de divorce.

Il a fait une demande de dommages et interêts.

If you want an equivalent to the English word "a demand," use *une exigence.*

brave - **brave**

The French adjective *brave* can mean brave. However, the most commonly used translation for the English word brave would **not** be the French word *brave*, but, instead, *courageux* or *intrépide.*

When it means brave, brave is placed after the noun that it's modifying, as in:

un homme très brave

On the other hand, *brave* is most often placed before the noun, in which case it means good, honest, simple, kind.

C'est un brave homme.

Ce sont de braves gens.

Un brave garçon.

In modern speech this is by far the most common usage.

vexer - **to vex**

vexations - **vexations**

vexant - **vexing**

> It's odd to have *vexer* as a *faux ami*. It is such a recognizable word that you would certainly guess that it means the same thing in English and in French. Unfortunately, it doesn't.
>
> In English, to vex means to annoy, to irritate, to anger, to frustrate.
>
> In French, *vexer* means to hurt someone's feelings or to offend them.
>
> *Se vexer* means to take offense, get upset or have your feelings hurt.
>
>> *Elle se vexe facilement.*
>>
>> *Il se vexe pour un rien.*
>>
>> *Il m'a beaucoup vexé.*
>
> In English vexations are irritations—in French *vexations* are humiliations.
>
>> *Elle est trop sensible pour supporter cette vexation.*
>
> And *vexant* means hurtful, wounding, humiliating.
>
> It's interesting that in one French dictionary I did find *vexant* listed with a secondary meaning of irritating and

annoying, (as in English). This meaning was listed as obsolescent in French.

Similarly, I did find to vex, in an English language source, with a secondary definition meaning to upset (as in French). This meaning was listed as obsolete in English.

I mention these not to confuse you but to demonstrate the common archaic source of the two words, even though they have now grown apart.

Remember that if someone says *"Je suis vexé!"* it doesn't mean that they are angry, it means they are hurt or upset.

If you are looking for a French equivalent of the English word "to vex," try *irriter, agacer, ennuyer, embêter, contrarier,* or *mettre en colère.*

éditer - to edit

The French verb *éditer* does mean to edit. However, it also means to publish, inspite of there being another perfectly good French word, *publier*, which also means to publish.

This second meaning of *éditer* is a *faux ami* and can be confusing.

versatile - versatile

Although these words are spelled exactly the same they have completely different meanings. The English word versatile means that something or someone is able to adapt to different usages or functions, or is able to serve in different ways.

On the other hand the French adjective *versatile* refers to a person or a mood and refers to the quality of being changeable or fickle and likely to change opinions or moods rapidly.

> *Cette foule peut être très versatile.*

> *Elle a un caractère versatile.*

If you want a French equivalent for the English word versatile, use *polyvalent* if you are talking about a tool, a room, or some other object.

If you are talking about a person, though, you can say something like *Elle a des talents variés,* or *Il a un esprit universel.* (Universel in this sense means all embracing, or covering everything.) Or just use *polyvalent* which is roughly translated as multipurpose.

My English language dictionary lists the origin of versatile, as coming from French in the early seventeenth century, with the meaning at the time being "inconstant or fluctuating." Since then the meaning has apparently stayed the same in French, but evolved and changed in English.

une injure - **an injury**
injurier - **to injure**

> In French, *une injure* is an insult or verbal abuse.

Ils en venaient aux injures - They came to insults over it.

Il m'a fait injure - He insulted me. (literary usage)

Il m'a injurié - He insulted me. (current usage)

Une injure is **not** an injury or a wound.

Injurier means to insult or verbally abuse.

If you want to say the English word "an injury" in French, use *une blessure*.

To find an equivalent to the English verb "to injure" in French, use *blesser*. To injure oneself is *se blesser*.

prétendre - **to pretend**
prétendu - **pretended**

In English, the most common meaning for "to pretend" is to make believe.

Prétendre, in French, does not mean to make believe.

Prétendre does mean to claim, as one's right, as in:

Il prétend à un meilleur salaire.

Or it can mean to simply claim or assert as in:

Elle prétend pouvoir le guérir - She claims to be able to cure him.

Elle prétend être fort habile.

Il prétend être de la noblesse - He claims to be of the nobility. (Note that in English this would mean he's making believe to be of the nobility, which is not at all the same thing.)

My French friends tell me that in current usage there can be a note of skepticism implied by the speaker who uses the word *prétendre*. In other words: "She claims to be able to cure him but who knows?" or "He claims to be of the nobility, but who knows?"

This brings it a little closer to the English word pretend, but it's not the same. If one pretends in English, it's **not** true, it's make-believe. If one uses *prétendre* in French, the claim may be true, but you have doubts.

Note that there is a vestige of these usages in English as in "the pretender to the throne" meaning someone claiming the throne. However, in English, "He pretends to" would be an archaic usage and practically its only usage is in this kind of a literary and historical context.

The past participle and adjective *prétendu* is used when something is claimed or asserted, but when one is skeptical about it. It's best translated as supposed, alleged or so called, as in

Une prétendue cantatrice.

If you are looking for a French eqivalent to "He is pretending," use *Il fait semblant.*

As an interesting aside, the English and French words pretension/*prétention* and pretentious/*prétentieux* come from the French *prétendre* (to claim or assert).

un délai - a delay

The French word *délai* means something like the time allowed, or the deadline for, or the period allowed. In some phrases it can look as if it has the same meaning as delay (*sans délai*, for example), but it's not really the same. Here are some examples:

> *Je vais livrer dans les délais.* - I will deliver on time, in the time allowed.

> *Il faut compter un délai de trois semaines.* - You must allow three weeks.

> *délai d'attente* - waiting period

> *délai de garantie* - term of guarantee, guarantee period

> *sans délai* - without any waiting period allowed, without delay

It's clear that the two words started off with a common ancestor but drifted apart over the centuries.

If you want to say in French that "There has been a delay," use *un retard*.

For "to delay" use *retarder, reporter* (to postpone) or *repousser*.

large -large

These words are deceptively similar in French and English but do not mean the same thing.

In English, large means big. If you say a large man you mean someone both tall and broad. If you are talking about an animal or a building you mean big. If you refer to "a large number of" it means "lots of."

Large doesn't usually have any of those meanings in French. In French, *large* usually means wide or broad.

> *Dix mètres de large* - ten meters in width.

> *Une large route* - a wide road

> *C'est plus haut que large* - It's higher than it is wide.

If you want to say large in the sense of big, use *grand* or *gros*. If you want to say large in the sense of tall, for a person use *grand*. For a building use *haut*.

If you want to say "a large number of...," say *"beaucoup de..."*

All that said, there are some cases where large and large overlap, especially when you are referring to something extended either literally or figuratively. For example:

> *un large cercle*

> *une large majorité*

> *dans une large mesure*

> *un esprit large*

> *un projet de large envergure* - a project of large scope

Also, *un pantalon large* is a baggy pair of pants.

There is also a French noun, *le large*, which means the open sea. Consequently, *au large de* means "off the shore of" and the idiom *prendre le large* means to run off or to escape—(literally, "to take to the sea").

assumer - to assume

Assumer and to assume have meanings that are like the partially overlapping circles that I discussed in the Introduction. The circles probably were originally totally superimposed, and identical in meaning, but they have slipped apart over the years.

In English, the most common reason of "to assume" is to suppose, to take for granted, to believe without evidence. *Assumer* **does not** have this meaning in French.

In both languages to assume means to take on (a responsibility, a debt, a charge, a role, an identity, a name, a pose, etc). This is the intersection of the two circles:

> *Je vais assumer la responsabilité.*

> *Il assume la dette.*

> *Il a assumé le rôle.*

In French, *assumer* also means to accept a consequence or a situation. To assume does not have this meaning in English.

> *Je m'assume comme je suis.*

49

Cette nouvelle doit être difficile à assumer.

J'assume les conséquences de mes actions.

librairie - **library**

This is a *faux-ami* that constantly confuses English speakers, (including myself). *Une librairie* is a bookstore. *Un libraire* is the person who runs *la librairie*—a bookseller.

If you want to say a library it's *une bibliothèque*, which, to add to your perplexity, also means a bookcase.

To summarize:

a bookstore = *une librairie*
a library = *une bibliothèque*
a bookcase = *une bibliothèque*

la lecture - **the lecture**

In English, a lecture is an educational talk or speech. It can also mean a scolding.

In French, *la lecture* doesn't have either of these meanings at all. It refers to the act of reading (but it doesn't imply that it's out loud, as it would in English).

la lecture d'un livre

Elle est absorbée dans la lecture d'un roman.

la lecture d'une partition (de musique)

la lecture silencieuse ou à voix haute - reading silently or out loud

Il essaie de donner le goût de la lecture aux étudiants.

un patron - a patron

In English a patron of a store is a customer, especially a regular customer. A patron of a hotel is a (frequent) guest.

A patron can also be someone who gives frequent support, financial or otherwise. For example: a patron of the arts.

Patron doesn't have either of these two meanings in French. In French, *un patron* is a boss, or a proprietor, of a business.

Le patron d'un restaurant.

Il faut demander à la patronne.

La patronne d'un hôtel.

Salut patron ! (Hi Boss!)

Finally *un patron* or *un saint patron* can refer to a patron saint as in English.

If you want to refer to a patron of a store in French, use *un client* or *un client régulier*. For a patron of the arts use *un mécène*.

In common usage the English word incoherent refers to speech that is disjointed and doesn't make sense. Incoherent speech can be secondary to illness, fever, brain injury, or even emotional upset, as in: "He was babbling incoherently."

A secondary usage, which is much less frequent, uses incoherent for a policy or theory that doesn't hold together logically or is self contradictory.

In French as well, the dictionary definition of *incohérent* is illogical and inconsistent, and from that you would think it means pretty much the same thing as the English word incoherent. However the overlapping circles of meaning have slipped a bit. *Incohérent* is used in ways that would jar the ear if they were in English. For example:

> *Qu'il ait fait cela n'est pas impossible mais c'est incohérent.*

This means that what he has done is either illogical or inconsistent with what one would expect. In English we would use "illogical" or "inconsistent" (depending on which we meant) instead of incoherent.

> *Elle est d'une humeur incohérente, qui produit parfois des baisers, parfois des coups.*

Here again we can figure out the meaning (inconsistent), but it sounds strange to us because it's a way of using incoherent that would not at all be normal usage in English.

What is different is that in English, incoherent has come to be used primarily for speech, or in a pinch for a policy or theory, which is disjointed or illogical. In French it is used generally for inconsistent or illogical, and specifically, as above, for behavior, in ways that are foreign to us.

abuser - **to abuse**

In English, to abuse power or authority means to take advantage of it and use it in a wrong or harmful way. To abuse alcohol or drugs means to use them to excess, to go beyond the limits. To abuse a person or child means to take advantage of a position of power to mistreat the person physically (or verbally), or to force oneself sexually on them.

Abuser, in French, can be used in all these same ways:

> *Il abuse de son pouvoir, de son autorité.*

> *Elle abuse de l'alcool.*

> *On croit qu'il a abusé de sa propre fille.*

However, *abuser* can also be used in a couple of senses which would be foreign to English. First of all it can mean to go too far in a social sense, or surpass the limits of politeness, as in:

> *Je ne vais pas rester longtemps. Je ne veux pas abuser.*

Abuser can also mean to fool someone—usually, but not

always, by taking advantage of their credulity. (French synonyms: *tromper, duper, berner*).

> *Il cherche à vous abuser.*

> *La ressemblance peut vous abuser.*

Similarly, *s'abuser* means to be mistaken (or to misunderstand).

> *Si je ne m'abuse, c'était l'année dernière.*

These usages can obviously confuse you if you are not aware of them.

éventuel - **eventual**

The French word *éventuel* is often misused and often misunderstood by English speakers.

In English, eventual means ultimate, final, concluding, as in "the eventual outcome." The French word *éventuel* doesn't mean that at all. It means possible in the sense that something may occur or ensue, depending on circumstances. For example:

> *Sa visite éventuelle* - His possible visit.

> *Une perte éventuelle* - A possible loss.

Similarly, *éventuellement* doesn't mean eventually, it means possibly in the sense of something which may occur depending on circumstances.

It's important to note that the French word *possible* also

means possible and it can be a synonym for éventuel, but it is usually used in a different sense: possible in the sense of something that can be done, something that is feasible:

> *Si c'est possible.* - If it's possible. If you can do it.

> *C'est pas possible !* - It can't be done. I can't do it. (langue familière)

> *C'est possible de rouler à cent cinquante ici.*

Éventuel, on the other hand, is restricted to possible in the sense of things which may occur.

If you want to say the English word eventual in French, say *final* or *définitif*.

If you want to say the English word eventually, say *finalement, enfin, en fin de compte,* or *par la suite.*

To say "They eventually arrived" say: *Ils sont finalement arrivés, Ils sont enfin arrivés,* or *Ils ont fini par arriver.*

caution - **caution**
cautionner - **to caution**

The French word *caution* has nothing to do with the English word. It refers to a guarantee, a security amount, or bail.

Similarly, *cautionner* means to guarantee, to vouch for, or to bail out.

If you want to say he acted with caution in French, use *avec prudence* or *avec précautions*.

If you want to say "We cautioned him (not to do it)," use *Nous l'avons mis en garde.*

un car - a car

This one is very simple: *Un car* is a bus or coach in French.

If you want to refer to an automobile, say *une voiture.*

ignorer - to ignore

Ignorer in French usually means to not know, to not be aware of. Only infrequently will it mean to ignore.

> *J'ignore qui elle est.* - I don't know who she is.

> *Il ignore tout ça.* - He doesn't know anything about that.

> *Je n'ignore pas les problèmes.* - I'm not unaware of the problems

On the other hand, in English, to ignore never means "to not know."

If you want to say "to ignore" in French, use *ne pas faire attention à* (advice, a red light or a person), or *ne pas répondre à* (a summons, a request, or an invitation).

l'évidence - **the evidence**

In English, evidence usually means proof, or has to do with facts or observations leading to a proof. For example: "The police have gathered a lot of evidence."

In French, *l'évidence* usually means obviousness, or what is so obvious that it needs no proof. It comes from the word *évident* (evident). Thus:

> *C'est une évidence !* - It's obvious.

> *Nier l'évidence* - To deny the obvious.

In both French and English *en évidence* and "in evidence" mean out in the open, or prominently displayed, although the nuance of meaning may be slightly different. For example:

> *On a laissé les livres bien en évidence sur la table.*

> Her artistic skill was much in evidence in spite of the few examples of her painting that we saw.

To say the English word "evidence" in French, use *preuve*.

évidemment - **evidently**

In English, evidently means plainly or obviously.

In French *évidemment* used to have the same meaning, but that usage is now archaic or obsolete.

57

In current usage, *évidemment* is used as a positive exclamation meaning: Of course! or Certainly! or Naturally! It is a synonym for *Bien sûr !* or *Bien entendu !*

> *Est-ce que vouz pouvez être là ? Évidemment !*

It can also mean incontestably, especially when it starts a sentence, as in:

> *Évidemment, elle a fait une erreur. !*

s'évader - to evade

In English, to evade means to avoid (responsibility, obligations, capture, responding to a question, etc.). It can also be used figuratively as in "Sleep continued to evade me."

The French word *s'évader*, on the other hand, means to escape (from prison, etc).

> *Il s'est évadé par la porte derrière le bar.*

It can be used, by extension, to mean to slip away (furtively), as a synonym of *s'éclipser*, or of *quitter* or *partir à la dérobée*.

> *Il s'est évadé du salon pour éviter de rencontre sa soeur.*

Finally, it can mean to escape figuratively as in:

> *Il essaie de s'évader de la réalité de sa condition.*

To say the English verb to evade in French use *éviter, esquiver* or *éluder*.

évasion - **evasion**

Similarly, while an evasion in English means an avoidance, dodging, sidestepping, or giving indirect answers meant to avoid the question, in French *une évasion* is an escape— either literally as in an escape from prison, or figuratively as in an escape from monotony, reality or everyday life.

To say the English word evasion in French, use *une dérobade* (for a responsibility or commitment), or *un subterfuge* (when it is a subterfuge).

la cure - **the cure**

A cure in English refers first to a treatment which can successfully bring an end to a disease condition and bring the restoration of good health, such as:

a cure for cancer

Second, it refers to the state of having good health restored.

She experienced a cure.

On the other hand, the French word, *une cure*, simply refers to a course of treatment.

une cure thermale

Il a fait une cure à Vichy.

Une cure is a course of treatment which has a certain length of time. It doesn't mean that you are "cured" when you finish it. You can take it again next year.

If you want to say the English noun cure in French, *le remède* comes pretty close.

As a curious aside, the idiom *n'avoir cure de quelque chose* means to not care about something. It has nothing to do with the usual meaning of *cure*.

> *Je n'ai cure de sa réputation.* - I don't care about his reputation

> *Je n'en ai cure.* - I don't care about it.

l'envie - the envy

The French word *envie* does mean envy, but that is just a small part of it's usage.

By far, the most common usage for *une envie* is a desire (or even a craving), as in:

> *J'ai envie de chocolat.*

> *J'ai envie de lire ce livre.*

> *Nous avons envie de manger dans ce restaurant.*

> *J'ai très envie de manger des myrtilles !* - I have a real craving for blueberries.

This usage, as you can see, has nothing at all to do with envy.

And, oddly, *une envie* can also mean a hangnail or a birthmark. You can tell, of course, from context.

s'amuser - to amuse yourself

Amuser does mean to amuse or entertain, as in:

Il a été très amusé par la blague

However the English expression "to amuse yourself" means to pass the time or occupy your time, rather than meaning to have a good time and to be amused.

I amused myself in reading the train schedules during the long wait at the station.

On the other hand, *s'amuser* has kept the meaning of having fun, enjoying yourself, or having a good time.

Je me suis bien amusé hier soir - I really had a good time last night.

If you want to say "I amused myself" in the sense of occupying your time, use *J'ai passé le temps*, or *Je me suis occupé à ...*

herbe - herb

In French, the most common meaning of *l'herbe* is plain old grass.

tondre l'herbe, couper l'herbe - to cut the grass

un brin d'herbe - a blade of grass

les mauvaises herbes - weeds

Une herbe can also mean an aromatic herb used for cooking, or a medicinal herb, as in English.

(*Les aromates* can also denote an aromatic herbes and spices.)

Finally, *herbe*, like grass in English, can mean marijuana in slang.

parasol - **parasol**
ombrelle - **umbrella**

In French:

Un parapluie is an umbrella.

Une ombrelle is a little hand held parasol.

Un parasol usually refers in modern speech to a large, semi-fixed, or fixed, sun shade, in an outdoor café, for instance. (*Un parasol* used to refer to a small hand held parasol as well, but that meaning has become obsolete.)

Thus to summarize:

A large fixed sunshade is *un parasol*

What we would call a parasol is *une ombrelle*.

What we would call an umbrella is *un parapluie*.

un physicien - **a physician**

In French, *un physicien* is a physicist. In English, a physician is a doctor.

If you want to say "a physician" in French, use *un médecin*.

une phrase - **a phrase**

While in English a phrase is a small group of words or an expression, in French, *une phrase* is a sentence.

If you want to say "a phrase" in French, *une expression* probably comes the closest.

user - **to use**

The French word *user* has two meanings. The first is to use, as in English. In this sense it's a synonym for *utiliser*, but it seems to be restricted to abstract things and it's written as *user de*, as in the examples below:

Il a usé de son influence.

Elle a usé de tendresse.

Il a usé d'un stratagème malin.

The second meaning of *user*, which is more common, is to use something until it is worn out, or more simply, to wear something out.

Elle porte une robe très usée.

assimiler à - **assimilate**

The French word *assimiler* does mean to assimilate but it has another completely different meaning as well.

I first encountered this second meaning while reading a political column in a French newspaper. I read something like:

> *Le parti Républicain peut être assimilé à un parti conservateur européen, mais il y a quelques différences.*

Clearly *assimilé à* didn't mean "assimilated to." I looked in my dictionary and found out that the second meaning for *assimiler à* is to liken to, to present as similar to, or to compare to.

More recently, in reading a *policier* translated into English from French, I came across the following:

> The attack on ... which had already been assimilated to the provocations of the extreme right wing...

I thought: That doesn't make sense—Oh! I see! The original French author must have written *qui avait déjà été assimilé à des provocations.*

It meant "which had already been likened to the provocations" but the English translator totally missed it. He or she didn't know the word *assimiler*, and translated it as if it was the English word assimilate!

That's why you are learning *faux amis*. So you don't make the same kind of mistake!

la cave - **the cave**
le cellier - **the cellar**

These are close enough to be recognizable, but they don't translate as you would expect.

A French *cave* is an English cellar.

> *la cave* or *la cave à vin* - the wine cellar

> *la cave à charbon* - the coal cellar

On the other hand, a French *cellier* is an English storeroom (which can be in the cellar, but usually isn't).

If you want to say the English word cave in French, you can't use *la cave*. It simply doesn't mean the same thing. Use *la grotte*.

le tourniquet - **the tourniquet**

This one really surprised me. After all, what else could *un tourniquet* be, except a tourniquet. Well, a lot of things, apparently.

Un tourniquet can indeed be a tourniquet when used in a medical context. However, *un tourniquet* is also used for a multitude of things that turn, including a turnstile, a garden sprinkler, and a revolving display table, among others.

I discovered this while reading a Maigret mystery when *le commissaire* entered a bookstore and looked at books displayed on *le tourniquet*. That really had me stumped until I discovered it was a revolving table.

un parent - **a parent**

The first couple of times I heard someone refer to *mon parent* when he obviously wasn't referring to his parent, were puzzling. I learned that in French *un parent* has two meanings.

First *un parent* means a parent as in English, a mother or a father.

The second meaning of *un parent* is a relative, usually a blood relative, even if distant.

You can almost always tell the difference by context, as in:

> *Mes parents sont sortis ce soir* - My parents went out tonight.

> *Je n'ai que trois parents vivants* - I have only three living relatives.

> *C'est une parente éloignée* - She's a distant relative.

> *Jean est un parent de ma femme* - Jean is a relative of my wife.

évoluer - **evolve**

Évoluer is another word that has more meanings in French than it does in English. It does mean to evolve, change, or progress by small transformation as in English.

La technologie a beaucoup évolué depuis...

However it has another meaning which is fairly unrelated. *Évoluer* also means to maneuver in the military sense, and can be used figuratively as in:

Beaucoup de couples évoluaient dans la salle de danse.

Les gens évoluaient autour la cheminée pour se réchauffer.

impotent - **impotent**

The French adjective *impotent* means crippled, unable to move, having much difficulty in moving, with French synonyms *infirme, invalide, paralytique.* It can refer to a person or to a body part. For example, one can speak of:

un bras impotent - a paralyzed arm

In English, the adjective impotent means powerless, or, when used in a sexual sense, unable to function.

If you want to say impotent in the sense of powerless (He felt impotent to do anything about it), use *impuissant.*

If you want to say impotent in the sexual sense, you use *impuissant* as well.

The French noun, *un impotent* (or *une impotente* for a woman), means someone who is disabled or crippled, unable to move about, or able to move about only with much difficulty.

impotence - **impotence**

The French **noun** *l'impotence* refers to the state of a person who is disabled or the state of a body part which is disabled or unable to function. It can be translated as the disability or the infirmity.

If you want to use the English noun "impotence" in the sense of powerlessness, use *impuissance*. If you wish to use it in the sexual sense, use *impuissance* as well.

un palace - **a palace**

This one may surprise you: *un palace* in French is a luxury hotel.

If you want to say the English word "a palace" in French, use *un palais*.

onéreux - **onerous**

In English, this adjective refers to a duty, responsibility or task, and means that it is burdensome or heavy.

> Having to make three long trips in a week seemed like an onerous task.

It used to have this meaning in French as well but this

sense of the word has become obsolete and is no longer used.

In modern French, the adjective *onéreux* refers to an expense and means costly. Some synonyms in French would be *cher, coûteux* and *dispendieux*.

Le loyer était trop onéreux.

The French idiom *à titre onéreux* means "on condition of payment being made."

un hasard - a hazard

In English a hazard is a danger, a peril, or a risk. For example:

a fire hazard

a health hazard

Ice is a hazard in this weather.

the hazards of smoking

In French, on the other hand, *hasard* is luck, chance or fate, but does not mean danger.

C'est un coup de hasard - a stroke of luck

par un coup de hasard - by mere chance, by coincidence

par un heureux hasard - by a lucky chance

Je suis arrivé ici par hasard - by accident, by chance

J'ai pris un chemin au hasard - at random

Remember that the French word *hasard* does **not** mean danger. If you want to say danger or risk in French, say *danger, péril*, or *risque*.

The English word hazard comes, of course, from the French word *hasard*, which comes from Turkish and Persian words meaning dice (hence, chance). You can see that both the English meaning of danger, peril or risk, and the French meaning of chance or luck came from the same original meaning but have drifted apart slightly over the centuries.

While the French and English nouns "hazard" and *"hasard"* now have different meanings, the verbs "to hazard" and *hasarder* have kept pretty much the same meanings.

Je vais hasarder une opinion - I'm going to hazard an opinion. (to venture, to risk)

Je ne veux pas hasarder beaucoup d'argent - I don't want to hazard much money (to risk)

un chandelier - a chandelier

In English, a chandelier is a decorative hanging ceiling light with multiple branches for bulbs.

In French, on the other hand, *un chandelier* is a candlestick holder (usually also with multiple branches), that we would call a candelabra.

If you want to refer to a ceiling light in French, say *un lustre.*

une casserole - **a casserole**

This one can confuse you a bit. In English a casserole is a (slowly cooked) stew which, or it can refer to a container that the stew may be cooked in (usually made of glass or earthenware).

> a beef casserole

> It was cooked in a casserole.

In French, however, *une casserole* has an entirely different meaning. *Une casserole* is a saucepan, that is used for cooking on the stovetop.

If you want to say a casserole referring to a stew, use un *ragoût* or *une daube.*

If you want to say a casserole referring to the container that the stew is cooked in, use *une cocotte.*

un pot - **a pot**

Here's another kitchen *faux ami.* Pot can have many meanings, both in English (belly, marijuana, etc.), and in French, but I am going to restrict my comments to the kitchen.

In English a pot can refer to a large round cylindrical (metal) pot for cooking, in which case it's *une marmite* in French.

On the other hand, if you are using "a pot" to refer to a saucepan it's *une casserole* in French, as we have just learned.

The French word *un pot*, (the "t" is not pronounced by the way), usually means a jar (for confiture for example), or some other kitchen container for liquids or foods. (*Un bocal* is another word for a jar).

Un pot can also refer to an (earthenware) jug containing milk or water. To give someone *un pot-de-vin* is to give them a bribe.

Finally, *un pot* can mean a flowerpot, which I guess could also be in the kitchen.

Un pot may rarely mean *une marmite* or cooking pot, as in English:

> *un pot-au-feu*

le plateau - the plateau

Since we are in the kitchen, while *un plateau*, in French, can mean a (geologic) plateau, as in English, the most common meaning of *un plateau* is a (kitchen) tray.

l'entrée - the entrée

To continue in the kitchen, the entrée, in American English

has come to mean the main course. *L'entrée* in French does **not** mean the main course. In common French usage *l'entrée* is the "entrance" into the meal—the small plate that we would call the appetizer.

It is really peculiar that this French word—adopted into American English—which so obviously means the beginning of the meal, has taken another sense.

Entrée, both in French and English has other meanings outside the kitchen, which meanings coincide for the most part. For example:

> He had entrée into the highest offices of the government

> *Il a ses entrées dans les bureaux les plus hauts...*

We are restricting ourselves, however, to the *faux ami* having to do with the kitchen.

le lard - **the lard**

Let's continue with another word from cooking. In English, "lard" refers to the fat from the abdomen of a pig that has been rendered and clarified and which is used in cooking. In slang it can also refer to excess fat on a person which is unattractive, as in:

> He's a ball of lard.

On the other hand, "bacon" in English refers to cured meat from the back or sides of a pig.

In French, *le lard* means bacon. *Le lard* does **not** mean lard. It refers to a layer of meat and fat rather than to rendered fat.

> *lard gras* - fatty bacon, mostly or almost entirely fat
>
> *lard maigre* - lean bacon, meat mixed with fat
>
> *omelette au lard* - bacon omelette

However, while we usually think of bacon in thinly sliced strips, in France it is often in chunks. Small diced *lard gras*, or bacon fat, is called *lardon*.

The French noun *le bacon* also refers to bacon, but in the form we are more used to: smoked lean salted pork (or *lard maigre fumé*), cut thin.

And finally, *la poitrine fumée* is another synonym for *le lard*, or the bacon

If you want to refer to English lard in French use *le saindoux*.

le change - the change

When it means the alteration or the act of becoming different, the English noun "the change" is translated *le changement*.

It's important to remember that you can't use the French noun *le change* as a synonym for the English noun change. If you want to talk about the change, meaning the alteration, in French, use *le changement*.

When talking about money, the English noun change refers to small coins:

I have a pocket full of change

If you want to talk about small change in French, use *la petite monnaie.*

j'ai trop de petite monnaie dans la poche.

When you ask for change for a large bill, it's la monnaie.

Est-ce que vous avez la monnaie sur un billet de cinquante euros ?

Pouvez-vous me faire la monnaie de cinquante euros?

After a purchase, in English the change refers to the difference between the money you tendered and the actual cost, in other words, what you will receive back.

I gave him three dollars in change.

To use change in this sense in French, you use la monnaie as well.

Gardez la monnaie ! - Keep the change

When talking about money, the French noun change means exchange (as in "foreign exchange").

un bureau de change

Le change est avantageux aujourd'hui - the rate of exchange is good today.

Le change du dollar est - The dollar exchange rate is

While you have to be careful with the French noun *le change*, the French verb *changer* usually can be used interchangeably with the English verb to change.

Elle a changé ses vêtements - She changed her clothes.

J'ai changé d'avis - I changed my mind.

Il faut changer la nappe - We need to change the tablecloth.

disposer de - to dispose of

There are three meanings of "to dispose."

1. In English, "to dispose of" usually means to get rid of.

He disposed of the garbage.

It can also mean to get rid of by handling decisively as in:

He disposed of the problem.

In French, *disposer de* never means "to get rid of." It always means to have at one's disposal.

Il peut disposer de cinq voitures.

les hommes dont je dispose - the men at my disposal

This is a true *faux ami.*

2. The French verb *disposer* (by itself, without the *de*), means to arrange or set out, and the English word dispose can also—although fairly uncommonly, have this same meaning:

> *Il faut disposer la chambre avec le lit à gauche.*

> *Comment est-ce que vous allez disposer les invités à la table ?*

> They disposed themselves around his office.

3. Finally, in English, "to dispose someone towards" means to make someone willing.

Similarly, "to be disposed towards" something means to be in the frame of mind to do something, as in:

> After what has happened she is not disposed to help him.

> He was disposed to agree.

In French *disposer* can have substantially the same sense. It can mean to put someone in the frame of mind to do something or to prepare someone psychologically for something, but it is used sometimes in nuanced ways in which it would not be used in English. For example:

> *Nous l'avons disposé à vous aider.* - We got him in a frame of mind to help you.

This would correspond with the English usage. But consider, on the other hand,

> *Le médecin a disposé le malade à mourir* - The doctor has prepared the sick person for death.

This is **not** a usage for dispose that one would likely see in English.

marcher - **to march**

Marcher in French has two general meanings, of which, to march in the military sense is only a very minor one.

First of all, *marcher* is the general word for to walk.

> *L'enfant a commencé à marcher tôt* - The child began walking early.

> *Il marche en boitant* - He limps when he walks.

> *Nous marchons à reculons* - We are walking backwards.

> *Les chats marchent à quatre pattes* - Cats walk on four legs.

Secondly, *marcher* means to function or to work, and can be used in a figurative sense as well, for instance referring to a plan.

> *Cette machine marche automatiquement* - That machine works automatically.

> *Le moteur ne marche pas* - The motor doesn't work.

Comment ça marche ? - How does that work?

Est-ce que les affaires marchent bien ? - How is business?

Est-ce que ça va marcher ? - Will that (plan, idea) work?

Qu'est-ce que vous pensez du plan ? Ça marche ! - That'll work!

Est-ce que ca marche ? - Do you agree? Will that work?

To march does **not** have either of these meanings in English.

mystifier - to mystify

The dictionary says that mystify came from the French *mystifier* in the early 19th century. However, in that relatively short time of just two hundred years, the two words have slipped apart in their meanings although they remain almost identical in appearance.

In English, the most common use of "to mystify someone" means to perplexe them, to puzzle them, to bewilder them, to baffle them.

> The disappearance of his wallet from the locked drawer mystified him.

In French, *mystifier quelqu'un* means to fool somebody, to take them in, to trick them or to "pull their leg." It can be either to laugh at their expense, or simply to fool them.

To mystify used to have this meaning as well in English but that usage has become obsolete and dated.

A good French synonym for *mystifier quelqu'un* is *faire marcher quelqu'un*.

balancer - to balance

In English, to balance something means to put or keep something steady and in equilibrium so that it won't fall.

He balanced the stone on top of the post.

It can also mean to compare or offset as in:

The costs are balanced against the benefits

In French, *balancer* does **not** mean the same things at all. In fact it comes close to being an opposite.

Instead of meaning keeping something steady, *balancer* means to swing (your arms or legs), to sway (your hips), to rock from side to side, or to oscillate.

Arrête de balancer les bras ! - Stop swinging your arms!

Il a balancé le bébé pour l'endormir - He rocked the baby to sleep.

Elle balance les hanches en marchant - She sways her hips while walking.

Les vagues balancent les bateaux à l'ancre - The waves rock the boats at anchor.

Balancer can also mean, in informal language, to toss or throw.

For example:

Balance-moi un coussin, s'il te plaît - Toss me a cushion, if you would.

Similarly *balancer* can mean to toss out or get rid of.

Il a balancé le noyau de la pêche par la fenêtre - He threw the peach pit out the window.

Elle a décidé de balancer ses vieux vêtements - She's decided to throw away her old clothes.

Il s'est balancé d'une fenêtre du quatrième étage - He threw himself out of a fourth floor window.

Balancer un compte means to balance an account, just like in English.

dresser - to dress

In English, to dress usually means to put clothes on oneself or someone else:

She dressed in a summer frock.

She dressed her daughter for the party.

To "dress a wound" can mean to treat and bandage the wound.

Less commonly, to "dress a fowl" can mean to clean and eviscerate it, which makes some sense as the dictionary points out that to dress comes from the Old French *dresser* meaning to arrange or prepare.

However, the modern French verb *dresser* doesn't have the same meanings as the English verb to dress. Not at all!

Dresser means to erect, put in a vertical position, and, by extending the meaning, to construct, or put up.

> *Ils ont dressé le mât* - They put up the mast.

> *Ils ont dresser le monument* - They raised the monument.

> *Elle a dressé la tête* - She raised her head.

> *Il s'est dressé* - He stood up.

> *Le chien a dressé les oreilles* - The dog pricked up it's ears.

Dresser can also mean to prepare or draw up a list or an inventory.

> *Dressez une liste pour moi, s'il vous plaît.*

If you want to say something about getting dressed in French, use *s'habiller*.

confiner - to confine

As you might expect, *confiner* does mean to confine, and *se confiner* is used in pretty much the same way as "to confine oneself" in English.

> *Il se confine chez soi* - He confines himself to his home.

> *Elle se confine à parler des choses banales* - She limits herself to speaking of ordinary things

However, *confiner* is very often used in another sense entirely, one which is not at all intuitive to an English speaker. In this sense *confiner* means to verge on or border on. For example:

> *Ses mots confinaient à la tendresse* - Her words were approaching tenderness.

> *Ses actes confinent à la folie* - His acts bordered on folly (or madness).

You may ask yourself, how did we go from "to confine" to "to verge on." It's not as illogical as it may appear. *Confiner* is used geographically to say that one country borders on another:

> *L'Italie confine à La France.*

One can see that, by bordering on France, Italy theoretically confines France in that direction.

The figurative sense (*confiner à la folie, etc.*) is an extension of this geographic usage, but the figurative sense is used much more frequently than the original geographic one.

errer - **to err**
errant - **errant**

In English, to err means to make a mistake. In French *errer* means simply to wander or rove as in:

> *Il errait dans les rues de Paris* - He was wandering through the streets of Paris.

Errer itself has none of the negative conotation of to err, however it is presumably by "wandering" off course that one makes *une erreur,* which does mean an error.

Errant also has a negative connotation in English as it means erring or straying from the proper course. An errant husband is an unfaithful one.

In French, again, *errant* simply means wandering as in:

> *des pensées errantes* - wandering thoughts

> *un chevalier errant* - a wandering knight

> *un chien errant* - a stray dog

> *la vie errante des nomades* - the wandering life of nomads

It is interesting to note that apparently both the English verb "to err," and the French verb *errer*, once had both meanings (to make a mistake and to wander). However to make a mistake is now listed as an obsolete usage of *errer* in French, and is no longer used.

Similarly, to wander in search of adventure is now listed as an obsolete usage of "to err" in English. Thus the two languages have gone off in different directions.

compulser - **to be compulsive, to compel**

When you first see the French verb *compulser* you are likely to be sure that it must have something to do with English words of the same general appearance. It doesn't.

The French *compulser* means to examine or consult notes, documents, or books (attentively).

Il a compulsé ses notes avant d'entrer.

The French words *compulsif* and *compulsion* are just alongside *compulser* in the *dictionnaire* and do mean compulsive and compulsion. *Compulser*, though coming from the same word stem, dances to its own tune.

le starter - **the starter**

In speaking about automobiles, the French noun *le starter* means the choke.

If you want to say "the starter" in French, use *le démarreur*.

un stage - a stage

In English, the noun "a stage" can have several meanings. First, it can refer to a period of development or a process:

> at that stage in my life

> The process was in an early stage.

> in a late stage of pregnancy

A stage is also a raised platform used for performances or plays, and there are other minor meanings for a stage as well (stage of a rocket, stage of a microscope, the profession of being an actor, etc).

In French, *un stage* does not have these meanings. Un stage means a training period:

> *Ma fille est partie pour un stage de trois semaines à Lyon.*

> *Cet été elle va faire un stage de poterie.*

> *Il faut faire un stage de formation.*

Note that while the French meaning of *un stage* also refers to a period of time, it is not at all the same meaning as in English. In English a stage can refer to any period of time during a development or process, while in French *un stage* is specifically a training period undergone by a person.

If you wish to refer in French to a stage in the sense of a period of time in a process, use un stade :

à ce stade de ma vie

à ce stade du projet

The processus était à un stade peu avancé.

You can also use *point* or *moment* :

à ce point de ma vie

à ce moment de ma vie

If you want to refer to the kind of stage which is a raised platform use *une estrade*—or if talking about coming "on stage" use *en scène*.

If you are talking about a stage of a journey, use *une étape*.

un toboggan - **a toboggan**

In French the most common use for *un toboggan* is to denote a slide for children in a playground. In commerce it can also be a slide for merchandise. In Canadian French *un toboggan* is a platform for carrying goods usually dragged along behind a horse. The word comes from the Algonquin language.

In English, a toboggan is a long thin sled for use in the snow. If you want to say the English word toboggan, meaning a sled, in French, use *une luge*.

un tissu - **a tissue**

Both the English and French words come from the French

verb *tisser*, to weave. In both languages *un tissu* or a tissue can refer to an intricate structure, "woven together," which can also be figurative, such as:

> a tissue of lies
>
> *un tissu de mensonges*
>
> *un tissu de bêtises* - a lot of nonsense
>
> *Le tissu urbain est plus dense dans les grandes villes*

In both languages *un tissu* or a tissue also may refer to body tissue. For example:

> epithelial tissue
>
> *tissu musculaire*
>
> *tissu nerveux*

However, the most common usage for the noun *tissu* in French is for textiles, fabrics and cloths, often woven, of course.

> *tissus de laine, de soie, de coton*
>
> *tissus de fibres synthétiques*

On the other hand, a tissue **never** means a textile or a fabric in English. Probably the most common meaning for "a tissue" in English is a piece of facial tissue or a paper handkerchief, or, to use a brand name: a Kleenex.

Conversely, *un tissu* **never** means a facial tissue or a paper handkerchief in French.

If you want to say "a tissue" in French in the sense of a facial tissue or a paper handkerchief, say *un mouchoir en papier or un kleenex.*

blesser - **to bless**

The verb *blesser* in French has nothing to do with the English verb to bless. In French, *blesser* means to wound. It can be used literally or figuratively.

> *Quand il est tombé il a été grièvement blessé.*
>
> *Est-ce que vous êtes blessé ?* - Are you hurt?
>
> *Ta suspicion m'a blessé* - Your suspicion wounded me (or hurt me).
>
> *Il m'a blessé au vif* - He cut me to the quick.

Remember that *Il m'a blessé* does **not** mean "He blessed me." It means "He wounded me," either literally or figuratively.

If you want to use the verb "to bless" in French, use *consacrer* or *bénir.*

blêmir - **to blemish**

The English verb, "to blemish" is listed in my dictionary as coming from the Old French verb *ble(s)mir*, meaning to injure, or to cause to turn pale. However, the two words "to blemish" and *blêmir* have drifted apart over the centuries.

(As an aside, the circumflex over the "ê," as in *blêmir*, often means that an "s" has been dropped, as the dictionary indicates one was dropped from *blesmir* to produce *blêmir*. For example consider *forêt*/forest and *hôpital*/hospital).

In English, to blemish means to mar, to stain, or to spoil the appearance of something which would otherwise be spotless. It can be used figuratively as well:

> There was only a small blemish on her complexion.

> His reputation was blemished by the accusation.

On the other hand, the French verb *blêmir* means to turn pale and it refers to a person.

> *Il a blêmi de peur.*

> *Elle a blêmi de rage.*

It can occasionally be used figuratively referring to a light which is fading or growing pale, as in:

> *Le jour blêmit.*

The English verb "to blemish" does **not** mean to grow pale.

The French verb *blêmir* does **not** mean to stain or tarnish.

If you want to use the English word "to blemish" in French, use *tacher* (or *entacher* if you are talking about honor or reputation). *Abîmer* or *gâcher* may also be suitable depending on what you are trying to say.

To say something is blemished you can say it is *taché* or that it has *une tache* or *des taches*.

You'll remember that the dictionary said that the Old French verb *ble(s)mir* had two related meanings: to injure and to cause to grow pale. It's interesting to note that the English verb, to blemish, seems to have held on to a form of "to injure" and has lost the sense of "to cause to grow pale," while the French verb, *blêmir*, seems to have done the opposite, holding on to "become pale" without any implication of injury.

lunatique - lunatic

The English adjective lunatic means crazy, foolish or absurd, as in:

> a lunatic scheme, a lunatic idea

On the other hand, the French adjective *lunatique* means moody, temperamental, with changeable unpredictable moods. It refers to a person:

> *Il est extravagant et un peu lunatique* - He's an immoderate person and also moody and unpredictable.

Both lunatic and *lunatique* come from the Old French *lunatique* and derive from the superstition that the moon (lune) made people moody and temporarily crazy. However, the meanings of the two words, as we have so often seen, have slipped a bit apart.

If you want to use the English word lunatic in French, use *fou*.

> *C'est un plan fou.*

extravagant - **extravagant**

The adjective extravagant has two meanings in English. The first meaning is immoderate, exceeding what is reasonable, going beyond reasonable limits, absurd, overly ornate. For example:

> extravagant remarks
>
> extravagant dress
>
> extravagant claims
>
> extravagant demands
>
> an extravagant price

The French adjective *extravagant* has this same first meaning and can be used interchangeably in this sense.

> *des prix extravagants* - unreasonable, immoderate
>
> *une tenue extravagante* - clothing (or behavior, depending on context), which is bizarre or beyond normal limits

des déclarations extravagantes - extravagant claims

However, in English, extravagant also means spending too much money, wasteful, lacking restraint in spending.

He is very extravagant and wastes a lot of money.

In French, *extravagant* does not mean wasteful and spending too much money. If you want to say that, use the French adjective *dépensier/dépensière* instead.

supplier - to supply

This one is very simple. The French verb *supplier* means to beseech, beg, implore, entreat. It has nothing to do with to supply.

Il m'a supplié de venir.

Écrivez-moi ! Je vous en supplie !

If you want to say "to supply" in French, use *fournir*.

ostensible - ostensible
ostensiblement - ostensibly

Ostensible is another very nice *faux ami*. Ostensible and *ostensible* are two words with identical spelling, which came from the same French word, but which have drifted apart in meaning to the extent that they verge on being opposites.

In English, ostensible is usually used as "the ostensible reason," or some similar wording, and it means the reason which is given as true, but is not necessarily true. There is an implication that the real reason may be being concealed.

> The ostensible reason for his visit to Paris was to visit his sister.

The adjective *ostensible*, in French, means not hidden, out in the open, overt, done with the intention of being seen openly. You can see that this is very different than the English meaning.

> *Ce sont des faits publics et ostensibles* - They are facts which are public and out in the open.

> *son mépris ostensible* - his open scorn

Similarly, ostensibly, in English, means apparently but not really or actually. At least not necessarily really or actually. The speaker doubts the truth of the facts.

> He's ostensibly in Paris to visit his sister.

> It seems he works for the government, ostensibly as some kind of lower level bureaucrat, but he may have some other job we don't know about.

And again, *ostensiblement*, in French means openly, overtly, out in the open.

> *Elle a même bâillé assez ostensiblement* - She even yawned fairly openly.

Il a ostensiblement montré son mépris - He showed his scorn openly.

If you want to say the English word ostensible in French, use *prétendu* or *apparent*.

If you want to use the English word ostensibly in French, use *prétendument, apparemment, en apparence*, or *il paraît que.*

Il paraît qu'il est à Paris pour voir sa soeur.

Il est à Paris apparemment pour voir sa soeur.

organique - **organic**

The French adjective *organique* means organic in most usages of the word, but it does **not** apply to "organic farming" or "organic foods." The French say *biologique*.

l'agriculture biologique - organic farming

Je cherche des pommes biologiques - I'm looking for organic apples.

Remember, **don't** say *organique* when you are looking for organic foods. Say *biologique*.

un bigot - **a bigot**

In English, while a fanatic or a zealot exhibits extreme enthusiasm and devotion to a belief or cause, a bigot is someone who not only is devoted to the cause or belief but shows contempt, intolerance and prejudice against those who are of other beliefs, or who belong to other groups.

In French *un bigot* is someone who is excessively religious and who has narrow beliefs—a religious zealot if you will—but it does **not** imply intolerance and sectarianism as it does in English.

Bigot can also be used as an adjective in French as in:

> *un homme bigot*
>
> *une éducation bigote*

but it doesn't mean bigoted, it means excessively religious.

If you want to say bigoted in French, in the English sense of the word, use *sectaire* or *intolérant*.

If you want to say "He is a bigot" in French, say *C'est un homme sectaire et intolérant.*

une apologie - **an apology**

The English noun, an apology, came in into the language in the 16th century from the French *apologie,* and originally had the meaning of a formal defense against an accusation.

Now, in English the primary meaning of "make an apology" has evolved to mean to say that you are sorry, to say that you regret what you have done, to excuse yourself, to present excuses.

An apology can also mean a sorry example of something as in:

He's a poor apology for a man.

And finally, in literary speech, an apology can still mean a defense as in "an exaggerated apology for rationalism."

In French, *une apologie* is still a speech or a piece of writing destined to defend something or to convince people of the correctness of something. It does not at all mean to make excuses or to say you are sorry.

Il a fait l'apologie du communisme - He made a defense of communism.

If you want to say "an apology" in the sense of excuses in French, **don't** say *une apologie*—use *les excuses*.

In order to say "to make an apology" use *faire des excuses* or *présenter des excuses*.

la robe - the robe

The most common use for the French word *la robe*, is for a woman's dress.

La robe can also mean a robe, like a judges robe, a priest's robe, or a bathrobe or dressing gown (*robe de chambre*).

On the other hand, the English noun, the robe, **never** means a woman's dress.

roman - **Roman**

romanesque - **Romanesque**

un romancier - **a romancer**

une romance - **a romance**

This is kind of complicated, so bear with me. We'll start with:

1. *roman* and Roman

The English adjective Roman means pertaining or coming from Rome, either the current city of Rome or the ancient Roman Empire.

> a Roman holiday
>
> a Roman road, a Roman arch

The French adjective, *roman*, most often refers to the medieval architectural style that we call Romanesque in English.

> *une église romane*

There is also a French noun, *un roman*, which used to traditionally refer to an old French type of literature, written in prose or verse, and involving romantic heroes, beautiful princesses, romantic love, and improbable, fabulous adventures.

However, *un roman* now most often simply means a novel.

> *un roman policier*

To translate the English word Roman, use *romain*. Lets go on now to:

2. *romanesque* and **Romanesque**

The adjective *romanesque*, which, as we just mentioned, refers to an architectural style in English, in French refers back to the traditional *roman*. In other words it implies sentimentality, heroes, improbability and romance.

> *Il y a quelque chose de romanesque dans cette aventure.*
>
> *une imagination romanesque*
>
> *un comportement romanesque* - romantic and unrealistic behavior

In addition, in literary usage *romanesque* can refer to the current day *roman*, or novel, as in:

> *l'oeuvre romanesque de Sartre* - Sartre's novels (as opposed to his plays, poetry, essays, and other writing).

Remember that the French word *romanesque* has nothing to do with the medieval architectural style that we call Romanesque.

3. *un romancier* and **a romancer**

Briefly, a romancer in English is someone prone to exaggeration and embellishment or, rarely, a writer of medieval romances.

In French, *un romancier* or *une romancière* is a novelist:

Simenon était un romancier très rénommé.

This now brings us to the adjectives:

4. *romantique* and romantic

Although **not** *faux amis*, these two words are discussed here because of their close relationship to the other words we have just been talking about, and because of the possibility of confusing them with these other words.

Romantic and *romantique* both refer to something arousing sentimentality, dealing with feelings of love, and moving the emotions in a somewhat idealized way.

> *le vieux quartier avec ses ruines, un endroit romantique*

You can see that *romanesque* and *romantique* may overlap a little, but don't really mean the same thing. A James Bond movie is *romanesque*. The play Romeo and Juliet is *romantique*.

Both *romantique* and Romantic (usually capitalized in English), may also refer to the movement of Romanticism at the end of the 18th and beginning of the 19th centuries.

> *les poètes romantiques*

> the Romantic poets

Finally we have:

5. *une romance* and a romance

In English, a romance is a story, film, or novel about love. In referring to a relationship, it is a love relationship, often emotional and also often passing.

> a summer romance

It can also refer to the simple charm of a place or situation.

> In the old town there was romance all around us.

In French, on the other hand, *une romance* is a sentimental ballad, of a type in vogue in the 18th and 19th centuries in France.

Romance seems like such a French concept that it is hard to believe that *romance*, in the sense we use it in English, is not a French word, but it's true.

If you want to refer to a romance (book, etc) in French, use *un roman d'amour* or *une histoire d'amour*.

If it's between people it's *une idylle d'amour, une aventure amoureuse,* or just *l'amour.*

If you are referring to ambiance, *poésie*, which can mean poetic charm, comes pretty close.

propre - proper

I'm sorry but this is another rather complicated *faux ami*.

The adjective "proper" has at least a half dozen usages in English:

> the proper tools for the job - suitable, correct

> give it to the proper person, the proper thing to say - correct

> proper behavior, proper dress - according to, or following, social standards and conventions.

> in Asia proper - as strictly defined

> He never went to a proper school - genuine

> a proper night's sleep - good

> a proper lady - real

> and more.

On the other hand, the two primary meanings of *propre* in French are clean and personal or one's own:

> *Utilise ta serviette propre* - Use your clean towel.

> *Utilise ta propre serviette* - Use your own towel.

> *Sa réputation n'est pas propre* - clean or spotless (figuratively)

> *mon propre vélo* - my own bike, my personal bike

Note that, in general, *propre* comes after the noun when

it means clean, and before the noun when it means personal.

L'amour-propre is a separate compound word meaning self-esteem (literally "love of oneself").

The English word proper does not mean either clean or personal or one's own.

Let's continue now to try to match other meanings of the French *propre* to those meanings of the English proper that we listed above.

First, the French word *propre* can mean suitable or proper, as in English:

> *Les conditions maintenant sont propres pour une discussion* - suitable, proper

> *C'est le terme propre* - most suitable

This is pretty much the only area where proper and propre have the same meaning. If we look at the other meanings of the English word proper, we find:

"Proper dress" in English means according to social standards. *Propre* does **not** mean according to social standards in French.

"a proper lady" (a real lady), "a proper school" (genuine), "a proper night's sleep" (good), "the proper person" (correct); all these usages in English would **not** be used in French!

"in the village proper" (in the village itself), can be expressed in French by *dans le village, proprement dit* (thus using a derivative of *propre*, at least).

Is there an overlap in meanings between proper and *propre*? Yes, but really just for the meaning "suitable." Proper and *propre* have slipped apart for other meanings so that now they barely overlap.

propriété - **propriety**

In English, the noun propriety refers to the state of behaving properly and conforming to conventionally accepted standards.

The French noun *propriété*, on the other hand, means property.

Thus this is a very simple *faux ami*.

If you want to say propriety in French, use *bienséance*.

comédien - **comedian**

In French *un comédien* or *une comédienne* is **not** a comedian. He or she is an actor or an actress in the theater.

Somewhat confusingly, *un acteur* or *une actrice* also can be an actor or an actress. But while *un comédien* is specifically an actor in the theater, *un acteur* or *une actrice* refers to an actor or actress in general, either in the theater or in the movies.

If you want to say the English word comedian in French say *un comique* or *une comique*.

normalement - **normally**

In French, *normalement* has three different possible senses.

First of all it can mean "in a normal fashion" (or "like a normal person"), as in English:

> *Hier soir, elle semblait un peu bizarre. Elle ne se comportait pas normalement* - Last evening she seemed a bit bizarre. She didn't behave normally.

> *Hier, tout s'est passé normalement* - Everything went in a normal fashion yesterday.

Secondly, *normalement* can mean "usually" or "ordinarily," again as in English:

> *Normalement elle travaille le samedi à la boulangerie* - Normally (ordinarily) she works Saturdays at the bakery.

However, *normalement* has a third, very common, meaning in French which is foreign to English. It is used to mean "provided everything goes well" or "if all goes well":

> *Normalement, nous arriverons vendredi* - If all goes as planned we will arrive Friday.

> *Normalement je serai là* - I expect to be there.

Some possible synonyms in French would be *Si tout va bien nous arriverons vendredi* and *En principe nous arriverons vendredi.*

"Normally" **does not** have this meaning in English. "Normally" does not mean "if all goes well."

un mécréant - a miscreant

Un mécréant and a miscreant both come from the Old French *mescreant*, meaning disbelieving or unbelieving.

In French, *un mécréant* still means an unbeliever or heathen. (*Mécréant*, used as an adjective is considered obsolescent).

In English, a miscreant has changed to mean a lawbreaker. (The meaning heretic is now listed as obsolete).

misérable - miserable

These are two words which still resemble each other greatly in meaning but which have slipped apart in nuance. In English, miserable has two meanings. It often means unhappy or sad.

> He has been miserable since the death of his daughter.

Secondly, it can refer to unpleasant conditions (which could make you feel unhappy or sad):

> It's a miserable day.

> My body feels miserable all over.

> He earns a miserable salary.

> He has a miserable life.

Finally, it can refer to something very small and insignificant:

> He got himself in trouble for a miserable little three dollars.

In French, *misérable* **never** means "unhappy or sad" as it does in English.

Misérable means arousing pity. This is not much different than the English meaning of being in unpleasant conditions:

> *Il vit dans des conditions misérables.*

> *Il a une vie misérable.*

Another related meaning for *misérable* is poor, impoverished, wretched, needy, or at the bottom of the social scale:

> *les populations misérables des pays du tiers-monde.*

> *les vêtements misérables* - shabby, worn, in rags, etc

Misérable can also mean insignificant, or arousing scorn. This also is little different than the English meaning:

> *un salaire misérable*

> *pour une misérable somme de deux euros*

> *Quel misérable !*

To review the differences: in French, *misérable* **never** means unhappy. Also, while both miserable and *misérable* can both be used for someone in impoverished circumstances, the meanings differ in nuance:

If you refer to a miserable population, the English words "a miserable population" say that the circumstances are unpleasant and that the people are unhappy, while the French words *une population misérable* says that the people are very poor. In English, miserable **doesn't** specifically mean poor or impoverished.

la misère - **the misery**

La misère has a number of meanings in French, but the primary meaning is extreme poverty or destitution.

> *Il est dans la misère* - He's poverty stricken, destitute.

> *Il vit dans la misère* - He's living in poverty.

> *un salaire de misère* - starvation wages

La misère can also mean troubles.

> *Il m'a apporté la misère.*

In English, misery does **not** mean poverty. The primary meaning of misery is sadness or suffering. As in French, misery can also mean misfortune.

> put him out of his misery

If you want to say the English word misery in French in the sense of sadness, use *la tristesse*.

If you want to say the English word misery in French in the sense of suffering, use *les souffrances* or *le supplice*.

truculent - **truculent**

While truculent in English means argumentative and looking for a fight, it has no such meaning in French.

In French, the same word, *truculent,* also refers to a person or style of speech, but means that the person is colorful, picturesque, bigger than life, and usually delightful. When it refers to speech it means colorful and perhaps racy speech.

> *C'était un personnage truculent* - He was a colorful personality.
>
> *des plaisanteries truculentes et poivrées* - colorful and spicy remarks or jokes.

Remember that the French word *truculent* does **not** mean argumentative. If you want to say the English word truculent in French, use *agressif.*

Note that "having a fierce appearance" is given as an obsolete meaning for the French *truculent,* indicating that the words were once much closer.

trépasser - **to trespass**

These two words have nothing in common. The French

word *trépasser* is a literary word that means to die. *Un trépassé* is a dead person.

If you want to use "to trespass" in French, a good starting place would be *entrer sans autorisation.*

trivial - **trivial**

In English trivial means of little importance, of little value, banal, commonplace.

In French the meaning *quelconque et insignifiant* for trivial has become obsolescent.

In current French, *trivial* has come to have a completely different meaning. It now means low, shocking, dirty, and vulgar and refers to speech or actions that are at the lowest levels and go against all societal norms. When referring to language *trivial* means vulgar and obscene.

engin - **engine**

In French, *un engin* is a machine, a tool, a device, or a contrivance, but it is not an engine or motor:

> *des pinces, des ciseaux et d"autres engins*

The way you say engine or motor in French is *moteur.* If you are talking about a railroad engine or locomotive, the French word is also *la locomotive.*

à-propos - **apropos**

These words have similar meanings but are used differently. In English, apropos is an adjective, meaning apt or appropriate:

> an apropos remark

> The remark was very apropos.

In French, *à-propos* is a noun and means aptness or appropriateness.

> *Il a repondu avec à-propos.*

Remember that you can't say "an apropos remark" in French, because *à-propos* is **not** an adjective.

In English "apropos of" can also be a preposition meaning with reference to:

> He made remarks apropos of the new plan.

In French *à propos de* means the same thing. (Note that in this case, à propos is two words and is not hyphenated).

> *Il a constaté, à propos du plan, que...*

> *Il a constaté, à propos de rien, que ...* - He remarked, not in reference to anything, that ... or, He remarked, for no good reason, that ...

les appointements - **the appointments**

In French, *les appointements* is only seen in the plural and means the salary. It has nothing to do with the English word appointments

Il a réçu ses appointements - He received his salary.

If you want to say "an appointment" in reference to a meeting, use *un rendez-vous*.

If you want to say "an appointment" in reference to being appointed to a position, use *une nomination*.

appointer - to appoint

In French, *appointer* means to pay a salary.

Il est appointé au mois - He is paid monthly.

Appointer can also mean to put a point on a pencil—in other words, to sharpen a pencil.

To say the English verb, to appoint, in French, use *nommer:*

Il m'a nommé directeur.

l'application - the application

In French, *une application* **never** means an application for a job or a university. It also **never** means to ask for something, as it can in English.

In French, *application* **does** refer to the application of paint to a wall, energy to a job, money to a project, to the application of oneself to one's work, or to the application of a rule or a law. All of these usages are as in English.

Il a fait deux applications de peinture.

Il travaille avec beaucoup de application.

C'est une bonne loi en théorie, mais il faut la mettre en application.

To say, in French, "to submit an application for a job," use *présenter sa candidature.*

To say, in French, "to submit an application (form)" to a university, use *un dossier d'inscription.*

For an application for membership, *une demande d'inscription.*

For an application for benefits or for money, use *un formulaire de demande.*

confus - **confused**

In French, the adjective *confus* can mean confused, as in English:

Il a des idées confuses.

However, most often, *confus* means embarrassed:

Je suis confus - I'm very embarrassed.

Elle était très confuse pour ce retard - She was very embarrassed because of the delay.

Confused **never** means embarrassed in English.

un bureau - **a bureau**

In both French and English a bureau can mean a desk.

In the United States, a bureau can be a government department, as in:

> The Federal Bureau of Investigation

> The Bureau of Indian Affairs

It **never** has this meaning in French.

In French, *un bureau* is the common name for an office.

> *Elle travaille dans son bureau* - She's working in her office.

It only rarely is used for an office in English, and then just for the limited and impersonal case of the distant office of a firm:

> The London bureau of the news agency.

It's **not** used in English for an individual person's office as it is in French.

fatal - **fatal**

In English, the adjective fatal means causing death or producing failure:

> He had received a fatal wound.

> There were fatal flaws in the plan.

In French, the adjective *fatal* has these same meanings:

Il a reçu un coup fatal.

un accident fatal

une blessure fatale

une erreur fatale

However, in French, a very common meaning for *fatal* is inevitable:

C'est presque fatal - It's almost inevitable.

C'est fatal que ça va tourner mal - It's inevitable that that will turn out badly.

Fatal is **not** used this way in English.

fatalement - **fatally**

In English, the meanings of the adverb fatally correspond to those of the English adjective fatal:

He was fatally wounded.

The plan was fatally flawed.

In French, *fatalement* only means inevitably and thus is totally a *faux ami*.

Cela devait fatalement tourner mal.

Synonyms in French are *forcément* and *inévitablement*.

To say the English word fatally in French, use *mortelle-ment* for a wound, and *irrémediablement* for a plan or project.

le sort - **the sort**

The French word, *le sort*, has nothing to do with the English word of the same spelling. *Le sort* means the fate, destiny.

> *Il était abandonné à son triste sort.*

> *Que sera son sort ?*

> *Le sort fait les parents, le choix fait les amis.*

> *Une ironie du sort.*

embrasser - **to embrace**

In English, to embrace means to hug, when it refers to people. In French this meaning is now obsolescent.

In current French, *embrasser* means to kiss when it refers to people.

> *Il l'a embrassé sur la joue/ sur la bouche* - He kissed her on the cheek, on the mouth.

> *Je t'embrasse* - In ending a letter or phone call this is a sign of affection.

In both languages the word can be used figuratively in the sense of embracing a philosophy, an idea, or another paradigm.

Il a embrassé sa nouvelle carrière.

To say "to hug someone" or "to give someone a hug" in French, use s*errer quelqu'un dans ses bras*, or, less frequently used, *étreindre quelqu'un.*

Il m'a serré dans ses bras.

Prends-moi dans tes bras - Embrace me. Give me a hug. Take me in your arms.

fastidieux - **fastidious**

In English, fastidious means very concerned with accuracy, detail or cleanliness.

In French, *fastidieux* refers to a task and implies that the task is boring and tedious because it's dull, monotonous, and long.

To say the English word fastidious in French, use *pointilleux* or *méticuleux.*

une idylle - **an idyll**

An idyll in English is a very picturesque, peaceful and happy scene or episode, often in a pastoral setting.

Une idylle in everyday French is a romance, a little amorous adventure, often naïve and innocent.

In literary French, *une idylle* can be a little poem on a pastoral and amorous subject.

l'issue - **the issue**

In French, *l'issue* is the way out, the exit, and figuratively, the way to get out of a difficulty. In ordinary English, an issue is **not** used in this way.

>*route sans issue* - dead end street

>*issue de secours* - emergency exit

>*La situation paraissait sans issue.*

In English, an issue can be a subject for debate or discussion, or a particular date of a periodical:

>the issue of global warming

>the December issue of the magazine

In rare instances one can use "issue out" as a verb in English to mean to exit.

le pétrole - **the petrol**

In British English, petrol is gasoline.

In French, *le pétrole* is petroleum.

>*pétrole brut* - crude oil

>*un puits de pétrole* - an oil well

To say gasoline, say *essence*.

un photographe - **a photograph**

In French, *un photographe* is a photographer.

To say a photograph in French, use *une photo or une photographie.*

un hôtel - **an hotel**

In French, *un hôtel* can mean an hotel.

> *Je vais rester à un hôtel ce soir.*

It can also mean a government building.

> *L'Hôtel de ville* - the Town Hall

Finally, *un hôtel* can mean a private mansion in the city.

In English, hotel has only the first of these meanings, which can be somewhat confusing when you are in Paris and find *Hôtels* all around you which are obviously not "hotels."

un récipient - **a recipient**

In English a recipient is someone who receives something.

In French, *un récipient* is a container.

To say recipient in French, use *bénéficiaire* (of a grant, etc), or *destinataire* (of a letter or package).

l'expérience - the experience

In French, *l'expérience* means the experience, as in English.

> *Elle a trois années d'expérience.*

> *L'expérience lui a montré que* - Experience has shown him that

> *C'était une mauvaise expérience.*

However in French, *l'expérience* has a second meaning which it does **not** have in English. *Une expérience* is an experiment or a trial, or a trying out.

> *faire une expérience* - to do an experiment

> *une expérience de chimie* - a chemistry experiment

> *Nous allons faire l'expérience de vivre ensemble* - We are going to experiment with living together, to try out living together.

Interestingly, there is a French verb, *expérimenter*, which does indeed mean to experiment or try out or to test.

> *Il faut expérimenter ce médicament sur les animaux.*

expérimenté - experimented

It's not enough that *une experience* in French can mean an experiment in English. We now discover that the meanings are exchanged in both directions and *expérimenté* in French means experienced!!

> *Ce n'est pas une jeune fille, c'est une femme expérimentée* - She's not a young girl, she's an experienced woman.

rester - **to rest**

In English, to rest means to take a break from activity or work, to allow recuperation.

> He rested after his long run.

To rest something, can also mean to place it or to lean it.

> He rested the ladder against the wall.

> His arm was resting on her shoulder.

> Her hopes rested on the new doctor.

In French, on the other hand, *rester* means to remain.

> *Il y a que trois jours qui reste avant...* - There are only three days remaining before...

> *Restez ici !* - Stay here!

> *Qu'est-ce qui reste à faire ?* - What remains to be done?

If you want to say the English verb "to rest" in French, use *reposer* or *appuyer*, depending on the sense of the word.

I need to rest - *Il faut me reposer.*

Her hopes rested on the doctor - *Ses espoirs reposait sur le médecin.*

He rested the ladder against the wall - *Il a appuyé l'échelle contre le mur.*

la réalisation - the realization

One meaning of realization in English is the fulfillment or the achievement of something.

It was the realization of her dreams.

However, by far the most common usage of "to have a realization" in English is to become aware of something.

He had the realization that he had made a mistake.

The **French** word, *réalisation* does not mean to become aware.

Le réalisation means the turning something into reality, the fulfillment, the achievement, the carrying out, the production (of a piece of work, a television show, etc), the creation (of a piece of art). In It is used much more broadly in these senses than it is in English.

la dernière réalisation de Cézanne - **Cezannes** last work of art

La réalisation de la coupure de bois va être en novembre.

Ce projet est en cours de réalisation.

Le pont de Millau est une belle réalisation.

Jean est le responsable de la réalisation du film - Jean is in charge of the production of the film.

If you want to say an equivalent to the English expression "to have a realization," in French, use *se rendre compte*.

Il s'est rendu compte qu'il a fait une erreur.

apostropher - **apostrophe**

In English an apostrophe is a punctuation mark, or in literature, an exclamatory passage in a speech or poem, addressed to someone who is not present.

In French, on the other hand, the verb *apostropher quelqu'un* means to shout at someone to get their attention, or to address someone sharply and rudely. It has nothing to do with the English meanings.

l'allure - **the allure**

In English, allure is the quality of being enticing, attractive, or fascinating.

In French, *l'allure* doesn't mean that at all. *L'allure* means the speed, or pace, and can also mean the bearing or style.

Il roule à toute allure - He's driving at full speed.

Les allures naturelles du cheval sont le pas, le trot, et le galop - The natural paces of a horse are walk, trot and gallop.

Il a fière allure - He holds himself proudly

Il a de l'allure - He has style, He has a certain elegance.

If you want to use the English expression "She has allure" in French, say *Elle est attirante, séduisante,* or *attrayante.*

dissimuler - to dissimulate

In English to dissimulate means to conceal and applies to feelings or thoughts.

He dissimulated his true feelings.

In French, dissimuler also means to conceal, but applies to the real world as well as the internal world. This makes it sometimes have a very foreign sound to us.

Quelque chose était dissimulé sous la couverture.

To dissimulate is simply **not** used this way in English.

subtiliser - subtle, to subtilise

In English, subtle means making use of fine distinctions or nuances. To subtilise is an obsolete English word meaning to make more subtle or refined.

The French verb, *subtiliser*, is similarly related to the French word *subtil* (subtle). Interestingly, *subtiliser* also has the same obsolete meaning as the English word to subtilise: to make more subtle. It can also mean to cut hairs or overdiscuss details.

However, in familiar French current usage, *subtiliser* means to pinch or swipe something adroitly on the sly.

> *Quelqu'un m'a subtilisé mon portfeuille dans le métro.*

This usage is common. Since it has nothing obvious to do with subtle, (except, perhaps, that someone had been subtle about swiping it), it may well cause confusion when you see or hear it.

un profane - **the profane**
profane - **profane**

In French, *un* or *une profane* is a person who is not initiated into an art, a science or a technique. For example:

> *Je n'ai jamais fait de ski. Je suis un profane* - I've never skied. I'm a beginner (or novice).

> *En peinture, c'est facile d'abuser le profane. Il est beaucoup plus difficile de fabriquer une pièce qui trompera un spécialiste* - In painting, it's easy to take advantage of the uninitiated. It's much harder to make a piece which will fool a specialist.

> *Il y a les choses que les profanes ne voient pas*

- There are the things that the uninitiated don't see.

In English, profane is never used in this sense. You can't even say "a profane" as a noun. In fact profane is rarely used as a noun at all. Only in an expression contrasting the religious and the secular, as in the "the sacred and the profane."

In French, *profane* as an adjective means uninitiated to a religion, and by extension, secular.

> *musique profane* - secular music

> *le monde profane* - the secular world

However, figuratively, and most commonly in current usage in French, *profane* means uninitiated to an art, science, sport, technique, etc.

> *Il est profane en ce sujet* - He doesn't know anything about the subject.

In English, profane as an adjective means either secular or irreverent. (I even found an obsolete usage of profane as meaning uninitiated into the mysteries of something. This would not be used in current day English, however.)

"To profane" and *profaner,* as verbs, both mean to treat something of a sacred character without respect and with scorn.

opiner - to opine

And for our final *faux ami* we have a fairly straightforward one:

To opine in English is a somewhat formal way of saying "to give an opinion."

In French, on the other hand, *opiner* means to agree, and *opiner de la tête* means to nod agreement. Often one shortens *opiner de la tête* to just *opiner* to mean nod in agreement.

Remember, *Il a opiné* doesn't mean he gave his opinion. It means he nodded in agreement.

If you want to say "to give an opinion" in French, use *exprimer l'avis* or *donner l'avis*.

I hope that you have found this book useful, and that it will help you in the future in reading, writing and speaking French. I must admit that I learned a great deal, as well, in writing it. I especially hope that you got as much pleasure from reading it as I received from writing it.

List of References

I used the following reference books to supplement my knowledge from everyday reading and conversation in the preparation of this book.

Dictionary 1.0.1, Apple Computer 2005

Harper Collins French Concise Dictionary, Second Edition, Harper Collins, 2000

Harrap's Shorter Dictionnaire, Anglais-Français Français-Anglais, 7th Edition, Chambers Harrap, 2004

Le Petit Larousse, Grand Format, Larousse, 2001

Le Petit Robert, Dictionnaire Alphabétique et Analogique de la Langue Française, Dictionnaires Le Robert, 1993

Webster's New World Dictionary, Second College Edition, Simon and Schuster, 1982

Alphabetical Listing of Faux Amis

Printed in the United States
69265LVS00003B/235

9 781587 367328